HOW DID IT HAPPEN?
THE GREAT DEPRESSION

R.G. Grant

LUCENT BOOKS

An imprint of Thomson Gale, a part of The Thomson Corporation

THOMSON

GALE

Detroit • New York • San Francisco • San Diego • New Haven, Conn.
Waterville, Maine • London • Munich

THOMSON

GALE

Produced by Arcturus Publishing Ltd
26/27 Bickels Yard
151–153 Bermondsey Street
London SE1 3HA

© 2005 Arcturus Publishing

Series concept: Alex Woolf
Editor: Philip de Ste. Croix
Designer: Stonecastle Graphics
Picture researcher: Thomas Mitchell

Picture credits:
All images copyright of Getty Images

Thomson and Star Logo are trademarks and Gale and Lucent
Books are registered trademarks used herein under license.

For more information, contact
Lucent Books
27500 Drake Rd.
Farmington Hills, MI 48331-3535
Or you can visit our Internet site at http://www.gale.com

LIBRARY OF CONGRESS CATALOGING-IN-PUBLICATION DATA

Grant, R. G.
  The Great Depression / by R.G. Grant.
    p. cm. — (How did it happen?)
  Includes bibliographical references and index.
  ISBN 1-59018-606-0 (hardcover : alk. paper)
  1. United States—History—1933–1945—Juvenile literature.
2. Depressions—1929—United States—Juvenile literature. 3.
United States—History—1919–1933—Juvenile literature. 4.
United States—Economic conditions—1918–1945—Juvenile
literature. 5. Economic history—1918–1945—Juvenile
literature. 6. World politics—1933–1945—Juvenile
literature. I. Title. II. Series.
E806.G733 2005
973.91—dc22
                                          2005029652

Printed in Singapore

Contents

1 A Troubled World

The Great Depression was a worldwide economic slump that produced mass unemployment and a collapse of world trade. The Depression was at its worst from 1929 to 1934, but the economic and political problems that caused it can be traced back to World War I (1914–1918), and these problems were not really resolved until World War II (1939–1945).

Before World War I, there was a capitalist world economy that, on the whole, functioned smoothly. Britain was the world's leading trading nation and acted as the world's banker, investing capital in many parts of the globe. Britain used this dominant position to maintain an orderly system of international finance and trade. The world's major industrial producers were the fast-growing United States and Germany, with Britain and France some way behind. A few other countries, such as Russia and Japan, were industrializing rapidly. Most of Asia, Africa, and South America supplied raw materials or food to the industrial countries.

The pre-1914 world was based on extreme inequality. Even within the richest countries, millions of people lived in abject poverty. Europe and North America ran the world economy for their own advantage. But the economic system was generally stable. Businessmen and industrialists felt they could invest money anywhere in the world with confidence. And this investment produced rapid economic growth—new railways, ports, and mines, and the opening up of fresh areas for farming.

More than 9 million soldiers lost their lives in World War I, many of them killed in the trench warfare of the Western Front. The industrial and financial resources of the world's leading economic powers were diverted to the business of destruction.

Disrupted by War

World War I brought massive disruption to the heart of the global economic system as the world's major industrial producers—including Britain, France, Germany, Russia, and, starting in 1917, the United States—devoted themselves to battle. The combatant countries concentrated their entire economic resources on the war effort, and their governments took unprecedented control over their national economies. Almost 10 million soldiers and uncounted millions of civilians died in Europe during the four years of conflict. By the end of the war, a defeated Germany was in political and economic chaos, with millions of its people on the brink of starvation. Russia had undergone a revolution that brought a Communist government to power. Britain and France had been effectively bankrupted, because they had paid for the arms that won the war with money borrowed from the United States.

Political and social unrest plagued Europe in the aftermath of the war. Germany was at times in a state of virtual civil war, with Communist uprisings and attempted coups by right-wing nationalists through the end of 1923. Russia underwent the horrors of civil war and widespread famine before, at the end of 1922, the Communists established the Soviet Union, the world's first anticapitalist state. Foreign investors and governments who had put money into Russia before the war lost it all as the Communists renounced the debts of the previous regime.

German government troops fight Communist revolutionaries, known as Spartacists, in armed conflict on the streets of Berlin in the winter of 1918–1919. The political and economic crisis that gripped Germany after World War I was a major obstacle to restoring a stable peacetime world economy.

VOICES FROM THE PAST

Global competition

Writing in Europe after World War I, German writer Oswald Spengler warned his fellow Europeans of the threat to their industries as production developed in other parts of the world:

"Today more or less everywhere—in the Far East, India, South America, South Africa—industrial regions are in being, or coming into being, which, owing to the low scale of wages, will face us with deadly competition."

Quoted in Mark Mazower, *Dark Continent* (Penguin, 1998)

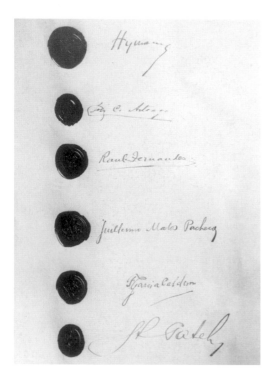

Problem of Reparations

Even when the postwar chaos died down, Europe remained haunted by the bitter aftermath of the conflict. In Germany, there was widespread hostility to the peace treaty imposed by the victors at Versailles in 1919. Germans especially resented the demand that Germany should pay reparations to the victors to compensate them for the cost of the war. Britain and France needed reparations payments partly because of their huge war debts to the United States—money taken from Germany would be used to pay back the Americans. The attempt to extract reparation payments from Germany embittered international relations in the postwar years, leading to the Franco-Belgian occupation of Germany's Ruhr district in 1923 and hyperinflation in Germany.

These signatures are on the Treaty of Versailles, the document that Germany was forced to sign at the peace conference held after the end of World War I. Many Germans blamed the terms of the treaty for causing their country's postwar economic and political difficulties.

TURNING POINT

The great German inflation

In January 1923, France and Belgium sent troops to occupy the Ruhr district, the industrial heartland of Germany. Their aim was to force the Germans to make the reparations payments imposed on them at the end of World War I. The Germans in the occupied area responded with passive resistance. Many industrial workers went on strike. In these chaotic conditions, hyperinflation took off and the value of the German currency collapsed. By November 1923, 600 billion German marks were equivalent to just one U.S. dollar. Forty billion marks were needed to buy what one mark would have bought in 1918. People's savings were wiped out—a person who had saved 68,000 marks in a lifetime of work found it was not enough to buy a postage stamp. Inflation ended in 1924 after foreign troops withdrew and a new mark was launched, but the experience of hyperinflation left many Germans bitter and insecure. It made them more ready to support political extremists in the future.

Britain Enters Depression

Although much more politically stable than Germany, Britain could not hope to restore the position it had held in the world economy before the war. Now a debtor nation, it could no longer dominate the world financial system. Its traditional industries such as ship-building, coal mining, and cotton textile production also failed to resume their prewar dominance in export markets. By the summer of 1921, 2 million workers were unemployed in Britain's industrial centers. According to historian John Stevenson, by June 1921 Britain had already "entered the years of the Depression."

The difficulties of British industry were one example of a worldwide problem in the postwar years. During the war, while the European countries devoted all their economic might to the armed struggle, other countries stepped in to take their place in the world market. Industrial production for export expanded in countries such as Japan and the United States, and in parts of the world ruled by Europeans as colonies—for example, British-ruled India. When the war ended and European industries turned once more from production of war materials to peacetime goods, there was more industrial capacity in the world than there was demand. This meant there were not enough customers to buy all that the world's factories and shipyards could produce.

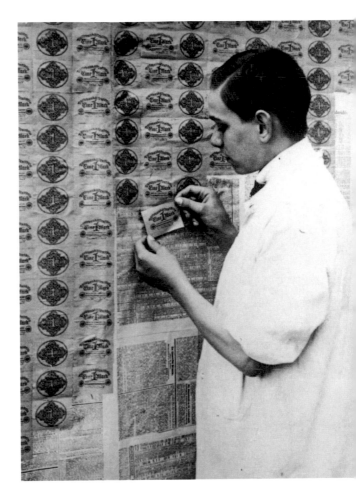

Hyperinflation in Germany in 1923 made banknotes so worthless that people used them to paper walls. Individuals who had savings in cash found their money had become almost valueless—a sum they had hoped to use to buy a house would barely cover the cost of a streetcar ticket.

Agricultural Overproduction

The problem was even more acute in agriculture. Even before the war, improvements in farming techniques and the opening up of new farmland had begun to lead to overproduction. More crops and meat were being produced globally, but the demand from consumers did not grow as fast. This situation was made worse by the war. Countries across the world, including Canada and the United States, increased agricultural production to levels that were higher than were needed once the war was over. As a result, in the 1920s, prices for agricultural goods worldwide tended to fall. Millions of people who worked the land were threatened with poverty.

Although American farmers suffered in the mounting agricultural crisis of the 1920s, on the whole the United States stood out as a remarkable success story in a world full of difficulty and disturbance. It had emerged from the war as the world's leading industrial and financial power. As its industries boomed through the 1920s, the United States was responsible for more than 40 percent of the world's total industrial production.

The first meeting of the Council of the League of Nations is held in Geneva, Switzerland, in November 1920. The United States refused to join the League, undermining its ability to promote international cooperation in the cause of peace and economic progress.

Power of the Dollar

Despite America's dominant position in the world economy, there was a strong current of opinion in the United States that favored isolationism—keeping the country out of involvement in the troubles and conflicts of the wider world. This was symbolized by the failure of the United States to join the League of Nations—the forerunner of the United Nations—in 1920. But America's economic power inevitably gave it great influence in shaping the world economy. Only the United States had capital to spare that could be invested to promote economic growth and stabilize the international financial system.

HOW DID IT HAPPEN?

American world leadership

After World War I, the United States replaced Britain as the world's leading financial power. It has often been said that U.S. isolationism—America's desire to turn its back on the outside world after the war—left the world economy leaderless. Historian Eric Hobsbawm wrote: "The world system, it could be argued, did not work, because, unlike Great Britain, which had been at its center before 1914, the USA did not much need the rest of the world and, therefore . . . did not bother to act as a global stabilizer."

But other historians of the period have disagreed. William A. Williams pointed out that self-interest caused the United States to involve itself in the wider world in the 1920s, so the U.S. government encouraged lending abroad by American companies and banks to keep the international economy afloat and promote America's export industries.

Eric Hobsbawm, *Age of Extremes* (Michael Joseph, 1994); Williams's views from Charles P. Kindelberger, *The World in Depression 1929–39* (Penguin, 1973)

In the mid-1920s, there appeared a serious chance that the world economy might get back on an even keel, achieving what was called at the time a "return to normalcy." The key was American money. In 1924, the American-backed Dawes Plan ended the immediate crisis over reparations, setting out an agreed-upon schedule for German payments. As investment from American banks and corporations flowed into Germany, the German mark was restored to value after the madness of the great inflation. American investment and American demand for raw materials and foodstuffs also stimulated economic growth elsewhere in the world, notably in South America.

In 1925, Britain returned to the gold standard—a method of fixing the value of a currency by relating each unit of currency to a certain amount of gold. This was effectively a gesture of confidence in the value of the pound (the British unit of currency) and was seen by many people as a sign that the orderly prewar world had returned. But the future of the world economy depended on the United States.

2 The Boom and the Crash

For many people in the United States, the 1920s were boom years. American industries flourished. Between 1922 and 1928 industrial output rose by 70 percent, an average of 10 percent a year. With new factories opening and old ones expanding, jobs were readily available and unemployment barely existed.

The major industrial growth area was the production of consumer goods for a mass market. Cars were the most striking single example. In 1914, there had been about half a million cars in the United States; by 1929 there were 26 million, one car for every five Americans. The United States had become the first country in which an average individual might expect to own an automobile. Electrical goods were another category that took off for the first time. Before World War I, fewer than one in five Americans had electricity in their homes; by 1927 about one in three did. This created a mass market for goods ranging from electric irons and

The Ford factory at Dearborn, Michigan, used production-line techniques to turn out inexpensive cars for a mass market in the 1920s. In 1929, the last year of the economic boom, the American automobile industry produced 5.6 million cars, about eight times as many as were manufactured in the whole of Europe.

VOICES FROM THE PAST

Presidential optimism

On December 4, 1928, President Calvin Coolidge—who was about to hand over the presidency to Herbert Hoover—told the U.S. Congress:

"No Congress of the United States ever assembled . . . has met with a more pleasing prospect than that which appears at the present time. . . . The great wealth created by our enterprise and industry, and saved by our economy, has had the widest distribution. . . . The country can regard the present with satisfaction and anticipate the future with optimism."

Eric Hobsbawm, *Age of Extremes* (Michael Joseph, 1994)

stoves to radios and vacuum cleaners. In effect, the United States had become the world's first fully developed consumer society—a society in which the production of what could be termed luxuries for the masses was the central economic activity.

Wealth and Poverty

Prosperity was clearly visible in many ways—for example, in the skyline of American cities, where skyscrapers shot up in increasing numbers and to ever greater heights. By 1929, in New York, the Chrysler Building was under construction, and planning was under way for the Empire State Building. Less visibly, however, substantial areas of American society were left out of the boom. For workers in the coal mines of Virginia or African Americans employed in the cotton fields of the South, the 1920s were a time of grinding poverty. In fact, while better-off Americans were buying cars and refrigerators, almost a third of the population had an income of less than $1,200 a year, a sum then considered the minimum on which a person could reasonably be expected to survive.

High above New York City, a construction worker tightens a bolt on the Empire State Building, with the newly completed Chrysler Building in the background. The construction of such skyscrapers in the late 1920s and early 1930s was the most visible sign of American prosperity.

Many of the poorest Americans were small farmers or farmhands. As in the rest of the world, agriculture in the United States suffered from overproduction. A combination of factors—including improved crops, new farm machinery, the bringing of new land into use, and the expansion of output during World War I—meant that American farmers could produce more than they could easily sell. As a result, the prices they were able to charge for their produce tended to fall, especially in the second half of the 1920s. For small farmers, falling prices were financially disastrous.

African Americans drag in bales of cotton to be weighed after a day's hard work in the cotton fields of Arkansas. Living in permanent poverty, workers like these were mostly little affected either by the boom of the 1920s or the Depression of the 1930s —they just went on being poor.

In some ways, a fall in agricultural prices was good for American industry. It meant cheaper food for workers and cheaper raw materials for factories. But the poverty of farmers and farmworkers—then more than two-fifths of the American population—was a serious problem for consumer industries. With no money to spare, the farmers could not afford to buy the goods the factories produced. Because a third of Americans were too poorly paid to afford automobiles, electrical goods, and other consumer goods, the consumer industries were bound to run out of customers sooner or later.

Buying on Credit

The other weak point of the 1920s boom in America was that it was based on easy credit. Loans were readily available at low interest and people took full advantage of the chance to borrow. Consumers borrowed to buy cars and electric stoves. Many farmers mortgaged their farms to raise loans from banks. By 1929, the debts of American farmers totaled about $10 billion. Obviously, people in debt were individually very vulnerable to an economic downturn. But the banks were also at risk. If, for example, farmers went bankrupt and their farms became virtually worthless, the banks would lose the money they had lent and might themselves be financially ruined.

Riskiest of all, people were borrowing money to invest in the stock market. From 1924 to 1929, buying shares seemed a sure way of making money, because share prices constantly went up. On average, they quadrupled in price over that period. At first the rise in share prices was modest and accurately reflected the increasing size or rising profits of businesses. But from 1927 onward, the rise in the markets turned into sheer speculation. Shares kept increasing in value simply because investors were always prepared to pay more for them, regardless of the success of the businesses that they were sharers in. Sharp traders started promoting shares in companies that did no business at all—buyers did not mind paying $5 for a share in a worthless company if they could sell the share to another investor a year later for $10. It was like a casino in which the gamblers never lost.

The New York Stock Exchange on Wall Street, the focus of the dramatic events of the crash of 1929, stands empty and ready for business. Millions of Americans who invested their money on Wall Street lost heavily when boom turned to bust.

Anxious crowds gather on Wall Street during the crash of October 1929. Investors could do little but wait for news as the shares they had bought with their savings dwindled in value.

By 1929, people were investing their life savings in the stock market, caught up in the fever of making easy money. Many of them bought shares on margin. This meant that an investor might pay as little as 10 percent of the price of the shares with his or her own money, borrowing the rest of the price from a broker—who in turn borrowed the money from a bank. In this way, with $10 a person could buy $100 worth of shares. But the deal was that if the value of the shares fell, the broker would either demand that the investor put up more money or would sell the investor out—that is, force the investor to sell the shares immediately to pay the broker off. This system was virtually guaranteed to turn any drop in share prices into an avalanche of forced sales.

The Boom Ends

By 1929, the weaknesses in the American economy—especially the mounting agricultural crisis and slowing industrial growth—were evident. In the atmosphere of feverish speculation on the stock exchange, all warning signs were ignored. There was a slight drop in the market in March 1929, but after this "wobble" speculation renewed at an ever more intense pitch. On September 3, there was a brief, sharp fall in share prices, but again it was quickly reversed. By mid-October, though, selling of shares had begun in earnest. Despite efforts by prominent American financiers to calm the situation with reassuring remarks, declining confidence turned to panic. On Black Thursday, October 24, there was a torrent of selling. With everyone wanting to sell shares and no one wanting to buy, share prices fell steeply as panicking investors sold for anything they could get. Over the following days people hoped for a possible recovery in prices, but on October 29, Black Tuesday, over 16 million shares were sold, many for next to nothing.

This collapse in share prices, known as "the Great Crash," shocked the American public. Many thousands of individuals who had put all their savings into shares or, even worse, had borrowed

In 1929, customers rush to withdraw their money from a bank that they have heard is about to fail. Thousands of American banks ran into difficulties and could not guarantee to repay people the money that they had put into their bank accounts.

TURNING POINT

Black Thursday

The American stock market crash began with heavy selling of shares late on Wednesday, October 23, 1929. When the stock market opened at 10 A.M. on the following day, Black Thursday, 1.6 million shares were sold in half an hour. The streets outside the New York Stock Exchange filled with anxious crowds. There were rumors of ruined speculators committing suicide. People's shocked faces showed, in the words of one eyewitness, "the dazed unbelief of men who have been robbed of their all." It was a fundamental blow to the confidence and optimism that had driven the economic boom of the 1920s.

Unemployed Americans line up for a charity handout of used clothes. Scenes such as these became common in 1930 as failing businesses laid off millions of workers, leaving them to survive on relief payments from city authorities or food and other essentials provided by charitable organizations.

money to buy shares, faced financial ruin as their shares were now worthless. Financial experts, however, spoke calmly of a market "correction," seeing the fall in prices as simply restoring share prices to a realistic level after a wave of speculation. Figures showed that on

average the crash only returned shares to the value they had held the previous year. Nor was it obvious that the United States was entering a major economic crisis. Although in 1930 industrial output fell and unemployment rose sharply, this was at first seen as merely a temporary situation. When President Herbert Hoover said in May 1930 that America had "passed the worst," he was expressing a widespread expectation that the economy would soon pick up again.

But neither the American stock market nor the American economy recovered. Instead, industrial output went on falling, unemployment went on rising, and share prices plummeted even further. By mid-1932, the average value of shares was a quarter of the level it had held at the end of 1929. The confidence in the future that had buoyed up the 1920s boom was gone. The Great Depression had arrived.

HOW DID IT HAPPEN?

The crash and the Depression

Economists and historians have taken varying views of the relationship between the Great Crash and the Depression. Some have seen the crash as a spectacular side effect of the onset of the Depression—shares falling in value because the American economy was going into decline. Economist Thomas Wilson, for example, wrote that the fall in share prices "reflected, in the main, the change which was already apparent in the industrial situation."

Others, by contrast, see the crash as having a decisive effect in causing the Depression by undermining confidence. Historian Maury Klein wrote: "The real problem lay . . . in the hearts and minds of the American people. The crash had struck a deadly, perhaps fatal blow [to] the American psyche."

Taking a middle way between these views, economic historian J.K. Galbraith wrote: "Had the economy been fundamentally sound in 1929 the effect of the great stock market crash might have been small. . . . But business in 1929 was not sound; on the contrary it was exceedingly fragile. It was vulnerable to the kind of blow it received from Wall Street."

Wilson and Galbraith quotes from J.K. Galbraith, *The Great Crash 1929* (Hamish Hamilton, 1955); Maury Klein, *Rainbow's End: The Crash of 1929* (Oxford, 2001)

3 In the Grip of Depression

A group of people in rural America gather around a car in 1930. Agricultural workers were among those hit by the Depression, and many of their children grew up in poverty as it took hold of the United States.

The downward spiral of the American economy in the early 1930s was spectacular. As factories closed, mass unemployment swept the United States. Around 5 million Americans were out of work by the end of 1930. In 1932, unemployment rose to over 12 million—one in four of the working population. Those lucky enough to have jobs faced wage cuts and only part-time work. Spending on consumer goods plummeted as people cut back on nonessential purchases. Between 1929 and 1932 sales of cars halved, while sales of electrical goods fell by about two-thirds. Meanwhile, prices for agricultural produce went into an ever steeper fall, bringing a wave of bankruptcies among farmers. The American banking system, based on large numbers of small banks often with inadequate resources, buckled as more and more people defaulted on loans and confidence slumped. Over a thousand banks failed in 1930 alone.

German Collapse

In Europe, as in the United States, industrial output fell sharply in the early 1930s and unemployment rose. Germany was the worst affected, undergoing a rapid economic collapse. German economic recovery in the 1920s had been based on American loans. When the slump came, Americans no longer had excess cash to invest abroad. The American money was pulled out, and German industrial output plummeted. Unemployment in Germany rose to 3 million in 1929 and around 5 million by 1931. The effect was less dramatic in Britain because the contrast with the 1920s was less stark, but the number of British unemployed escalated from 2 million in 1929 to 3 million in 1931.

Inevitably, the slump in industrialized states in Europe and North America badly affected those countries that supplied them with raw materials or with foodstuffs. Many of those countries had already been

VOICES FROM THE PAST

Blow from afar

Thousands of workers in Chile, South America, lived by mining copper for export to the United States. When the Depression hit the United States, the copper mines closed down. A Chilean miner expressed his sense of shock:

"The crisis took us by surprise. It was as if you were walking in the street and something hits you and you are simply stunned. New York was far away, but when your own patron [boss] tells you that you no longer have a job, that the work's over, well, that's the moment you go into shock."

Quoted in Godfrey Hodgson, *People's Century* (BBC Books, 1995)

Unemployed British men line up at a labor exchange in 1930. In order to receive their unemployment benefit payments from the state, the unemployed had to "sign on" regularly at the exchange, signifying that they were available for work, even though there were no jobs to be had.

hit by falling prices. As industries cut back on production, they needed fewer imported raw materials, and hard-up consumers bought less imported food, drinks, or luxury products. Workers in the Japanese silk industry found themselves out of work because fewer American women bought silk stockings. Nitrate producers in Chile, supplying fertilizer to American farmers, were thrown out of work as U.S. farming declined. Workers on rubber plantations in Malaya suffered because, as car production declined, so did the demand for rubber for tires. In Brazil, so much coffee produced for export remained unsold that coffee beans were used as fuel for steam locomotives on the railways.

Members of Adolf Hitler's Nazi Party in Germany listen to one of their leader's speeches. Millions of Germans gave Hitler their support in the early 1930s because they believed his extreme nationalist policies were the best answer to economic collapse and mass unemployment.

Balancing Budgets

There was no coordinated international response to the deepening world depression. Most economic experts in Europe and North America were reluctant to admit that anything exceptional was happening. They took the view that occasional short-term slumps were a natural part of the functioning of a capitalist economy. The experts advised governments to balance their budgets—in other words, make sure that government expenditures equaled government income from taxes and fees—and keep the value of the national currency fixed. If governments did this, it was argued, the world would soon pull out of the Depression and resume economic growth.

So the reaction of governments to falling output and mounting unemployment was generally to cut spending and raise taxes in order to keep national finances stable. But balancing budgets in the Depression was difficult because reduced economic activity meant reduced income from taxes. At the same time, rising unemployment —at least in countries such as Britain and Germany with state unemployment benefit plans—meant that governments had to spend more to meet the cost of benefits.

The worsening economic situation inevitably put a strain on political systems as governments struggled to cope with the crisis. In South America, the governments of ten countries were overthrown in

TURNING POINT

The Invergordon mutiny

In September 1931, the British government, faced with a mounting financial crisis, introduced measures to cut spending. The income of everyone paid by the state was slashed. This included the unemployed, whose benefits were cut by 10 percent; teachers, whose pay was reduced by 15 percent; and members of the armed forces, some of whom faced a 25 percent pay cut. On September 15, sailors at Invergordon naval base in Scotland refused duty in protest of the cuts. When news of this mutiny in the Royal Navy spread, it undermined what little confidence foreign investors still had in Britain. As foreigners withdrew their money, the value of the pound had a natural tendency to fall because nobody wanted it. The government was unable to resist this financial pressure and was forced to abandon the sacred gold standard. The value of the pound dropped by a quarter on foreign exchange markets. Meanwhile, the government announced that all pay and benefit cuts would be limited to a maximum of 10 percent, and the sailors quietly returned to duty after two days.

This woman was injured during a demonstration against unemployment in Bristol, England, in February 1932. Most such protests were organized by the National Unemployed Workers Movement, many of whose leaders were Communists. On the whole, in Britain demonstrations were rarely violent and political extremists of the right and left won little popular support.

two years. In Germany, political life, which had been temporarily stabilized during the years of relative prosperity in 1924–1928, was once more torn apart as both the Communists and Adolf Hitler's right-wing nationalist Nazis attracted mass support by proposing radical solutions to the economic crisis.

European Financial Crisis

The crisis in Europe came to a head dramatically in the spring and summer of 1931. In May of that year, the Creditanstalt bank in Austria closed down. It was by far the largest bank in the country, controlling investment in most of Austrian industry. As a result of the Creditanstalt collapse, panic swept through Germany and Central Europe as people rushed to withdraw their money from banks they feared might go under. In the summer of 1931, the financial crisis engulfed Britain. In August, British prime minister Ramsay MacDonald established a coalition national government to carry through spending cuts. Even so, Britain was forced to abandon the gold standard that fixed the value of the pound. Many other countries followed Britain's lead. The battle to uphold a world economic system based on fixed exchange rates and stable currencies had been lost.

Once the gold standard was abandoned, the value of one national currency against another—for example, how many U.S. dollars were equivalent to a certain number of British pounds—was no longer fixed and predictable. As a result, it was much more difficult for importers in one country to pay for goods from another country. This contributed to a collapse in world trade, which shrank by an astonishing 60 percent between 1929 and 1933. A bad situation was made worse by the imposition of tariffs. These were taxes levied by countries on imports of particular goods. Their purpose, apart from raising revenue, was to protect a nation's industry and agriculture from foreign competition by making imported goods more expensive to buy. The United States led the way with the Hawley-Smoot Tariff Act of 1930, which imposed heavy tariffs on agricultural imports to protect hard-pressed American farmers. Almost all other countries followed suit, imposing their own tariffs to protect the most vital and

American president Herbert Hoover took action to boost the economy as the Depression worsened, but his policies failed to halt rising unemployment or to counter increasing poverty. By the election year of 1932, Hoover appeared to many Americans as both heartless and incompetent.

VOICES FROM THE PAST

Failed fathers

Larry Van Dusen was a teenager in America during the Depression. He described the strain his father's unemployment put on family life:

"One of the most common things—and it certainly happened to me—was this feeling of your father's failure. That somehow he hadn't beaten the rap. Sure, things were tough, but why should I be the kid who had to put a piece of cardboard into the sole of my shoe to go to school? . . . The shock, the confusion, the hurt that many kids felt about their fathers not being able to provide for them . . . . reflected itself very often in bitter quarrels between father and son."

Quoted in Studs Terkel, *Hard Times* (Pantheon Books, 1986)

vulnerable areas of their national economies. Imposing tariffs has been described as a "beggar-my-neighbor" policy—an attempt to improve one's own country's situation at the expense of everyone else's. It was a sign that, in the absence of any coordinated international response to the economic crisis, each country was going to seek its own national solution.

Hoover Reacts

This was certainly true in the United States. Hoover had taken positive action to boost the American economy. In 1930, he cut taxes and tried to persuade businessmen to stop cutting wages, so people would have money in their pockets to spend. In 1931, he set up the Reconstruction Finance Corporation, which provided federal money to boost construction projects and prop up banks. And federal cash was provided to buy surplus farm produce in an effort to stop the fall in farm prices. But Hoover also wanted to balance the federal budget and maintain the value of the dollar. With this in view, in 1932 he raised taxes and interest rates and cut spending, even though the Depression was still deepening.

By 1932, it was obvious that America was in the grip of a major crisis. It was visible in the shantytowns, ironically dubbed "Hoovervilles," that sprang up across the United States, where people lived in shacks made of old oil cans and tires. These housed people who had been evicted from their homes because they could no longer afford the rent—there were about a quarter of a million evictions in 1932—or bankrupt small farmers whose mortgaged farms had been repossessed by banks. "Panhandlers" on the streets begged for small change, and thousands of "hobos"—many of them teenagers who had left home because they were too much of a burden for their families to feed—roamed the country, traveling illegally on freight trains in search of temporary work.

In the early 1930s, thousands of poverty-stricken Americans were living in makeshift shacks in shantytowns on the outskirts of cities. These shantytowns were dubbed "Hoovervilles" after the president who was held responsible for the depressed state of the American economy.

America in Crisis

Whereas in major European countries there was generally some form of nationwide unemployment benefit or welfare payments, in the United States the unemployed or impoverished had to depend on

One initiative to provide relief for the unemployed in New York in the early 1930s was giving people boxes of apples to sell on the street. Women were often first to lose their jobs when the Depression set in, especially if they were married, as there was much male prejudice against married women working.

charities or on state or city authorities. Hoover opposed giving any federal money to the unemployed. But the charities and local authorities could not cope with a situation in which 12–13 million people were out of work. At all levels of government in the United States, falling revenues resulting from the Depression caused a mounting financial crisis. By 1932, many public authorities did not have enough money to pay the wages of employees such as teachers, let alone relief payments for the unemployed. When relief failed, poverty was acute. A woman in Chicago in 1932 witnessed "50 men fighting over a barrel of garbage outside the back door of a restaurant."

In the summer of 1932 the mounting sense of anger and betrayal felt by large areas of American society found dramatic expression in the Bonus Army protest. This was organized by unemployed war veterans—men who had fought in the U.S. Army in World War I. They demanded immediate payment of a bonus that had been granted to them by the government in 1924, but was not scheduled to be paid in full until 1945. The protesters, more than 10,000 strong, set up camp in Washington, D.C., vowing not to leave until the bonus was paid. Hoover and the U.S. Congress were equally determined not to pay up. On July 28, the U.S. Army was ordered to attack the Bonus Army encampment and drive the protesters out.

This whole episode confirmed a growing impression among the American public that Hoover was both incompetent to deal with the economic crisis and heartless in his response to the people's suffering. In the presidential election the following autumn, Americans voted in droves for Hoover's opponent, Democratic candidate Franklin D. Roosevelt. A dramatic new phase in the struggle to cope with the Depression was set to begin.

HOW DID IT HAPPEN?

Government policies and the Depression

?

In the 1930s, British economist John Maynard Keynes argued that, by cutting spending and raising taxes in the Depression, governments had made the situation much worse. He argued that the Depression was mainly caused by lack of demand for goods. Governments, he argued, should have cut taxes and increased spending to stimulate the economy, even if this meant not balancing their budgets.

However, this view has been hotly contested by advocates of liberal capitalism such as American economist Milton Friedman. They argue that the Depression was unnecessarily harsh and prolonged because many forms of government interference prevented the natural workings of a capitalist economy that would otherwise have soon restored prosperity.

Almost everyone agrees, though, that policy makers in the early 1930s had little idea how to respond to the crisis. As historian Eric Hobsbawm wrote: "Never did a ship founder with a captain and crew more ignorant of the reasons for its misfortune or more impotent to do anything about it."

Eric Hobsbawm, *Industry and Empire* (Penguin, 1968)

U.S. soldiers in gas masks advance to clear Bonus Army protesters out of Washington, D.C., in July 1932. The protesters, unemployed U.S. Army veterans who had served in World War I, won a great deal of public sympathy, and their harsh treatment further discredited Hoover's administration.

4 Fighting Back

Franklin D. Roosevelt was inaugurated as U.S. president in March 1933. He had won the presidential election with two main promises. One was to repeal Prohibition, ending the ban on alcohol imposed in the United States in 1919. The other was to introduce a "New Deal" to conquer the Depression. He had promised to concern himself with "the forgotten man at the bottom of the economic pyramid." Repealing Prohibition was easily done by passing a new law. But coping with the Depression was another matter.

VOICES FROM THE PAST

Roosevelt's inauguration speech

Opening his inauguration speech on March 3, 1933, Franklin D. Roosevelt told the American people:

"Let me assert my firm belief that the only thing we have to fear is fear itself—nameless, unreasoning, unjustified terror which paralyzes needed efforts to convert retreat into advance." The speech ended with Roosevelt announcing his intention of asking Congress *"for broad executive powers to wage a war against the emergency, as great as the power that would be given to me if we were in fact invaded by a foreign foe."*

Quoted in Martin Gilbert, *A History of the Twentieth Century* (HarperCollins, 1997)

Roosevelt and his advisers had confused and contradictory ideas about how to get America working again. For example, Roosevelt was very conservative in his attitude to public finance. One of his first acts as president was to cut the wages of federal employees in an effort to balance the budget. Yet his New Deal policies led to a sharp rise in federal spending and a totally unplanned budget deficit.

The Human Touch

Although not skilled at economics, the new president brought to the White House an immense dynamism, an openness to fresh thinking and initiatives of all kinds, and a human warmth that inspired confidence. His regular radio broadcasts, known as "fireside chats"

because of their intimate style, created a direct human bond with millions of Americans. One Chicago doctor later said: "It was the hopeful voice of FDR that got this thing out of the swamps."

From the outset, Roosevelt displayed a flair for affecting the national mood. In March 1933, the United States was in the thick of a major banking crisis. Across the country, investors had stormed banks, desperate to withdraw their savings, which they feared they would lose if the bank failed. Many states had declared "bank holidays," closing all banks to stop this panic withdrawal of funds. Immediately after his election, in a deliberately dramatic gesture, Roosevelt declared a nationwide bank holiday. Every bank in the United States was closed. A law was rushed through Congress stating that no bank would be allowed to reopen unless the federal authorities were sure that it was reliable. Roosevelt then spoke to Americans on the radio, assuring them that putting their money in banks was safe. Over the following weeks almost all banks reopened, and confidence was restored.

President Franklin D. Roosevelt talks into radio microphones, giving one of the regular "fireside chats" in which he spoke directly to the American people. Roosevelt projected a personal warmth that gave many Americans comfort and renewed confidence in difficult times.

Trying to Restore Growth

The major challenge facing Roosevelt was to spark economic growth. He hoped to do this by reversing the spiral of falling prices and falling wages. In agriculture, the federal government tried to persuade farmers to limit production in order to cut surpluses and stop falling prices. Cotton farmers were paid to take land out of production. The government organized the slaughter of millions of piglets to avoid a surplus of pork. In industry, the National Recovery Administration (NRA) tried to get businesses to stop cutting wages and prices and to abandon certain bad practices—for instance, to stop employing child labor. Many businesses across the United States agreed to implement the voluntary NRA codes and displayed the NRA Blue Eagle badge that promised they were following the new rules.

In practice, the New Deal industrial and agricultural recovery policies were of limited effect. The NRA encouraged large businesses to make price-fixing agreements that guaranteed their profits, encouraging them not to compete with one another. They took advantage of this policy, while largely ignoring pressure to improve wages or working conditions. Similarly, in agriculture, large-scale farmers succeeded in profiting from government payments, but there was no improvement for small farm owners or tenant farmers. Overall, there was a gradual economic recovery in the first four years of Roosevelt's presidency, with growth of about 10 percent a year, but this was not enough to solve the problem of mass unemployment. Roughly one in eight Americans was still unemployed in 1937.

This 1933 cartoon, entitled "Spirit of the New Deal," shows how the National Recovery Administration (NRA) was supposed to work, with employers and employees brought together in the warm embrace of Uncle Sam, symbol of the United States. In practice, employers often took advantage of aspects of the NRA that suited them, while doing little or nothing for their workers.

Work for the Unemployed

Since mass unemployment persisted, the New Deal measures aimed to directly benefit the unemployed were of immense importance. One of Roosevelt's first acts was to provide federal funding for bankrupt state and city unemployment relief programs. Although the amount of relief people received varied enormously depending on where they lived, for many people the provision of federal funds was a lifeline.

There were also large-scale federal work programs for the unemployed. For example, the Civilian Conservation

Corps (CCC) was exclusively for young people. At its height, the CCC set 2.5 million youths to work on rural projects such as tree planting. The Civil Works Administration (CWA) and the Works Progress Administration (WPA) provided employment for adults, mostly performing road-building and other construction work, but also doing a wide range of other activities, from running libraries and theaters to painting murals on public buildings. These programs operated on a large scale—the CWA employed more than 4 million people in January 1934. Although undoubtedly some of the work they provided was a "boondoggle"—a word coined to describe a pointless and unnecessary job—the New Deal programs gave millions of unemployed people a sense of worth and purpose, as well as pay well above what they would have received on welfare.

Young people at a Civilian Conservation Corps (CCC) camp in Virginia pose with the tools they are using on a tree-planting program. The CCC was a highly successful part of the New Deal, giving millions of young unemployed Americans something useful to do, as well as benefiting the environment.

TURNING POINT

The first hundred days

From the second week in March to mid-June 1933—the first hundred days of Roosevelt's presidency—the U.S. Congress passed more new legislation than in any similar period before or since. This included the Emergency Banking Act, which set out to restore confidence in the banking system, and the Farm Relief Act, intended to tackle the crisis in agriculture. Other acts established the Civilian Conservation Corps to provide work for unemployed young people; the Public Works Administration to promote major construction projects; the Tennessee Valley Authority to develop a depressed region of the South; and the National Recovery Administration, intended to get industry back on its feet. These measures were described by a journalist at the time as a "whirlwind of changes in the old order." Whatever their practical impact, they created an impression of dynamism that lifted the mood of much of the American nation.

Roosevelt's policies met with a lot of opposition, partly from people who thought he should be more radical, but more especially from the wealthy and from big business. He was criticized for increasing the size and power of the federal administration. By 1935, the U.S. Supreme Court had declared several New Deal policies unconstitutional, including the NRA, and they had to be abandoned. Undeterred, Roosevelt pressed ahead with a fresh wave of even more radical legislation in 1935, sometimes called the Second New Deal. New measures included the Wagner Act, which gave federal support to workers who formed trade unions, and the Social Security Act, which introduced old-age pensions and welfare benefits. In 1936, the American people had their chance to pass judgment on the New Deal in a presidential election. Roosevelt won an overwhelming majority of the popular vote.

Nazis in Power

Roosevelt was not the only new leader to come to power in 1933 committed to ending

The Tennessee Valley Authority (TVA), set up under the New Deal, was a federally funded development program designed to bring electricity and other forms of economic progress to a large area of the rural southern United States. Here work is beginning on one of the dams that were a central feature of the TVA program.

VOICES FROM THE PAST

Grateful to Roosevelt

Hank Oettinger, a worker from Wisconsin, remembered when local men who had been unemployed for years got their first payment for working on a New Deal program in 1933:

"It was on a Friday. Everyone had gotten his [pay] check. The first check a lot of them had in three years. . . . I never saw such a change of attitude. Instead of walking around feeling dreary and looking sorrowful, everybody was joyous. . . . They had money in their pockets for the first time. If Roosevelt had run for president the next day, he'd have gone in by 100 percent."

Studs Terkel, *Hard Times* (Pantheon Books, 1986)

Roosevelt acknowledges applause at his inauguration ceremony in 1937 after being reelected for a second term in the White House. In all, Roosevelt won four presidential elections—in 1932, 1936, 1940, and 1944—a record that will never be equaled, since the U.S. Constitution now limits any president to a maximum of two terms in office.

unemployment. In Germany, Nazi Party leader Adolf Hitler became chancellor (head of government) in January of that year. The economic policies of Hitler's government were in some ways similar to the American New Deal. Large-scale, state-funded construction projects—including the building of the first autobahns (highways) provided work, while an immense propaganda effort restored public confidence in Germany's future. Nazi policy differed sharply from Roosevelt's New Deal, however, in its emphasis on military spending. Hitler's expansion of Germany's armed forces both employed men directly as soldiers and created thousands of new jobs in armaments factories.

German dictator Adolf Hitler presides over the official opening of construction work on an autobahn (highway). Road-building was one of the state-funded projects that generated employment in Germany after Hitler's Nazis came to power in 1933.

The major difference between Nazi policies and the American New Deal, however, was that Nazi policies were implemented by force. Hitler imposed a dictatorship. Independent trade unions were brutally suppressed and their leaders sent to concentration camps. In 1935, unemployment was made illegal. If a man did not have a job, he had to perform compulsory national labor service, working on the land or on building military installations. Women were pressured to leave jobs and return to what Nazis saw as their proper place in the home, freeing up jobs for men. Jews, whom the Nazis blamed for all Germany's misfortunes, were forced out of good jobs, which became available to other Germans. Although based on a loss of political freedom, Nazi policies unquestionably solved the problem of unemployment. To

In the Soviet Union, a board advertises the progress being made in fulfilling the objectives of the government's five-year economic plan in the early 1930s. The apparent success of the Soviet state-owned economy in generating rapid industrial growth made many people in the West believe that state control and economic planning were the secret to ending the Depression.

many Germans in the 1930s, this seemed an economic miracle, making Hitler's dictatorship immensely popular.

Growth in Stalin's Russia

Another answer to the Depression had been found in the Soviet Union. There, the Communist dictator, Joseph Stalin, presided over rapid industrialization and urbanization at the height of the Depression. The Soviet capital, Moscow, was the world's fastest-growing city in the 1930s. The Soviet economy was organized by the state, which directed resources and workers to the fulfillment of ambitious production targets laid down in a series of four- or five-year economic plans. As in Nazi Germany, unemployment was a crime.

In the early 1930s, the growth of industrial production in the Soviet Union was in stark contrast to the sharp falls in capitalist industrial countries. Many people in the 1930s believed that the Soviet Union was proving the superiority of communism to capitalism. Yet, although Soviet industrial growth in the 1930s was real, it was bought at an appalling cost. Millions of Soviet citizens died in mass famines, and millions more were used as slave labor in concentration camps.

Country	Change in industrial output 1929–1932
France	- 25.6%
Germany	- 40.8%
Italy	- 22.7%
Britain	- 11.4%
United States	- 44.7%
Soviet Union	+ 66.7%

Living and working conditions for ordinary Soviet workers were far worse than those of average workers in western Europe or North America.

But even if the view of Communist success in the 1930s was an illusion, the view that capitalism had failed was understandable. Although different national governments adopted different economic policies, they had all given up on attempts to re-create the stable, harmonious, global capitalist economy considered normal before 1914. The conditions created by the Depression had been accepted as the new normality.

HOW DID IT HAPPEN?

Conservative or radical New Deal

Some left-wing historians have criticized the New Deal for being too conservative and saving big business at the expense of the poor. Barton Bernstein wrote: "The New Deal . . . failed to raise the impoverished, it failed to redistribute income, to extend equality."

Others have pointed out that Roosevelt himself always claimed to have conservative aims. For example, in 1936, he said: "It was this administration which saved the system of private profit and free enterprise after it had been dragged to the brink of ruin."

But historian Carl Degler asserted that the New Deal was radical—even revolutionary—in an American context, because of the way it extended the scope of government. Degler said that the New Deal made the state into "a vigorous and dynamic force in society energizing and, if necessary, supplanting private enterprise when the general welfare required it." The New Deal has also been praised for social inclusiveness. David M. Kennedy wrote that Roosevelt succeeded in his aim of making "a country in which no one is left out," giving countless Americans "a sense of security, and with it a sense of having a stake in their country."

Barton Bernstein, *Towards a New Past* (Pantheon, 1968); Carl Degler, *Out of Our Past* (Harper & Row, 1984); David M. Kennedy, *Freedom from Fear* (Oxford University Press, 1999)

5 The Flawed Recovery

By 1934, the worst of the worldwide Depression was over. As conventional economic experts had predicted, a recovery took place regardless of what policies governments pursued. In Britain, for example, where no radical economic policies to combat the slump had been attempted, a sharp rebound brought industrial output back up to 1920s levels. It is probable that much of the fall in unemployment that happened in Germany and the United States between 1933 and 1935 was also caused by a spontaneous recovery in economic activity—a natural consequence of what economists call "economic cycles"—rather than by the New Deal or Hitler's dictatorship.

Depressed Trade

But the recovery did not mean that the problems of depressed world trade and mass unemployment were solved. Throughout the 1930s, world trade stayed far below the level it had been at before the Depression. There was no restoration of a unified world economy based on free trade and national currencies with a fixed value (as with the gold standard). A World Economic Conference, held in London in 1933, achieved nothing after the United States refused to take part in an effort to restore the fixed value of currencies, which would have made international trade easier. In response to the Depression, the United States, like other countries, had turned its back on the search for economic progress based on international cooperation.

Countries that had extreme nationalist governments were openly opposed to the return of free trade. The German Nazi regime, for example, sought as far as possible to make Germany economically self-sufficient. Ideally, Germany wanted to produce everything required to satisfy its own needs, and especially the needs of its armed forces. Where this was not possible, it imported goods from foreign countries that it directly or indirectly dominated. Some eastern European countries—for example, Romania—were made to sign trade deals in which they agreed to supply Germany with essential materials such as oil and foodstuffs in return for German

In the 1930s, New Zealand sheep farmers like these could sell their mutton or wool only to Britain or other countries within the British Empire. Trading outside the nations that used the British pound sterling as a currency was almost impossible for countries within the empire.

industrial goods. Such deals were highly favorable to Germany, but the other countries could not refuse them because they feared Germany's military might.

Even countries such as Britain and France, which in principle still believed that world trade could and should be restored, in practice no longer traded freely. Britain's trade, for example, was largely restricted to countries that would trade using the British currency, the pound sterling, in their transactions. Britain made its overseas empire into a protected trade area, ensuring that countries inside the empire, such as Australia and New Zealand, exported most of their produce to Britain and bought most of their imported goods from Britain, too.

Persistent Unemployment

In addition to world trade failing to recover through the 1930s, areas of mass unemployment still persisted. In Britain, for example, throughout the decade high levels of unemployment continued in parts of the country dependent on industries such as coal mining, shipbuilding, and cotton textiles. The experience of unemployment in such areas was especially grim as it struck entire communities—in towns such as Jarrow in northern England, a large majority of people were without work for years on end. The plight of the British unemployed was effectively

Men from the town of Jarrow in northern England march to London in protest of long-term unemployment in 1936. Jarrow was a shipbuilding town, devastated by the collapse in orders for British-built ships—a result both of foreign competition and of the decline in world trade, which meant fewer cargo ships were needed.

VOICES FROM THE PAST

Unemployment in Britain

In 1933, author J.B. Priestley visited Hebburn, a town on the Tyne River in northern England. He wrote:

"Idle men—and not unemployable casual labourers but skilled men—hung about the streets, waiting for Doomsday. Nothing, it seemed, would ever happen here again. . . . It is not merely that two-thirds of the town is living on the edge of destitution, tightening its belt another notch every month or two, but that its self-respect is vanishing."

J.B. Priestley, *English Journey* (Heinemann, 1934)

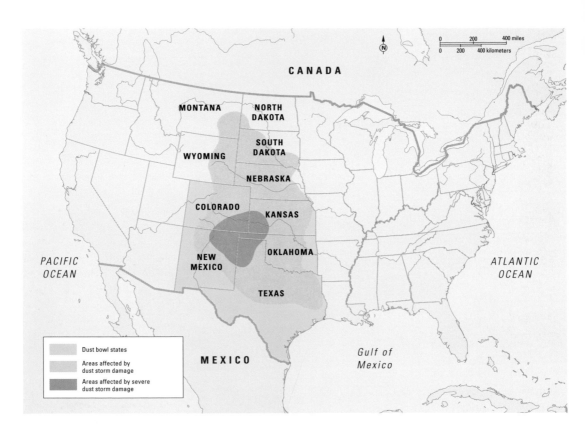

CANADA

MONTANA
NORTH DAKOTA
SOUTH DAKOTA
WYOMING
NEBRASKA
COLORADO
KANSAS
NEW MEXICO
OKLAHOMA
TEXAS

PACIFIC OCEAN

ATLANTIC OCEAN

MEXICO

Gulf of Mexico

Dust bowl states
Areas affected by dust storm damage
Areas affected by severe dust storm damage

The effects of drought and bad farming practices led to wind erosion of topsoil across a swath of the Great Plains in the 1930s, creating the "dust bowl," an ecological and economic disaster.

publicized in 1936 by a march of two hundred men from Jarrow to London to deliver a petition to Parliament. But although the marchers were regarded with great sympathy, they failed to persuade Britain's political leaders to take radical action.

In the United States, unemployment not only persisted but actually worsened again during Roosevelt's second term in office. In the second half of 1937, there was sharp recession in American industry. In some areas, such as automobile manufacture and steel production, much of the gain made in the recovery since 1933 was lost in a few months. As industrial production fell, unemployment rose. Although production picked up somewhat in the last two years of the decade, in 1939 there were 9 million unemployed in the United States, compared with the 12–13 million when the New Deal began in the depths of the Depression in 1933.

High unemployment reflected the failure of American industry to make a true recovery. The problems of American agriculture remained just as acute. Some of the worst poverty in America was found among African American rural workers in the southern United States. All tenant farmers—those who did not own their own land—had a tough time in the 1930s. The fate of the "Okies," who migrated

TURNING POINT

The Dust Bowl

The southern Great Plains of the United States—especially Oklahoma and Kansas—suffered from intensive farming that was unsuited to the relatively poor soil. It made the topsoil vulnerable to wind erosion whenever there was a drought, and droughts were not uncommon. In the early 1930s, the soil was stripped from large areas in a series of massive dust storms. One such storm, in May 1934, carried dust as far as the distant cities of Boston and New York. The once-valued farmland became a "dust bowl" where nothing would grow. About 300,000 farmers—known as "Okies" after Oklahoma, although they came from other states as well—were forced to migrate. Most headed west toward California in search of work.

This photo was taken by Dorothea Lange, a photographer employed by the Farm Security Administration to document the suffering of America's rural poor. It shows a migrant worker and her children in a camp in California, where like many others she had gone in search of work as a fruit-picker.

from the plains of the dust bowl to become badly paid fruit-pickers on the farms of California, was especially harsh. Roosevelt set up the Farm Security Administration (FSA) in 1937 in an attempt to tackle rural poverty. It had some effect, giving loans to poor farmers and providing improved housing for Okies in California. But many of the rural poor found their own solution by migrating to the cities. In particular, black migration from the rural South to America's northern cities grew in scale through the 1920s and 1930s.

Adjusting to Change

In America, the experience of the Depression and the New Deal led to the spread of radical political action and ideas. Millions of Americans joined trade unions for the first time in the 1930s, and there were widespread strikes over pay, working conditions, and the right to recognition of unions by employers. In 1937, some 400,000 Americans were involved in sitdown strikes—that is, strikes in which workers occupied their workplace. Despite the Roosevelt administration's general support for unionization, strikers were often attacked by armed strikebreakers in the pay of the employers, or by police and the National Guard sent in by state or city authorities.

The 1930s were not, however, a time of nothing but political conflict, unemployment, and poverty. They were also a time when technological progress—from the spread of the use of electricity and the first introduction of plastics and nylon goods, to movies with color and sound—brought real improvement to many people's lives. The low prices that created poverty for farmers across the world made imported food cheap for town and city dwellers with jobs. In Britain, while old industries such as shipbuilding and cotton textiles declined, new industries sprang up, mostly in the Midlands and southern England, producing cars, electrical goods, and aircraft. On the whole, workers in the new industries were better paid and better housed than working people had been a generation earlier.

Essentially, by the late 1930s the world was getting on with its business in the new conditions that the Depression had brought. There seemed no reason why high unemployment and shrunken world trade should not continue into the future. Some of Roosevelt's advisers had privately concluded that unemployment in America would never again fall below 6 million.

Workers occupy the General Motors plant in Flint, Michigan, during the wave of sitdown strikes in 1936–1937. The strikes were hard-fought, with outbreaks of violence between strikers and police or vigilantes paid by the employers. These men are making clear their hostility to "scabs"—those who refuse to join the strike. The dummy hanging from the window represents their view on company "stools," or stool-pigeons, paid to spy on the strikers.

HOW DID IT HAPPEN?

Capitalism in question

In the 1930s, the failure of a full economic recovery to materialize was widely believed to show the fundamental failure of capitalism as an economic system. Capitalism was condemned as irrational, because factories closed and land lay idle while millions of poor people lacked the basic necessities of life. Left-wing groups in the United States called for "a scientifically planned economic system." Factories and farms should be directed by the government to produce what people needed—"production for use instead of profit."

It is more common nowadays, however, to see the failure of recovery as a consequence of a breakdown in international cooperation, which undermined the capitalist system. For example, journalist Alan Shipman wrote in 2002: "Recovery was . . . delayed because nations could not work together to rekindle activity, instead trying to revive their own economies by raising trade barriers and devaluing their currencies."

Socialist quotes in Anthony Badger, *The New Deal* (Macmillan, 1989); Alan Shipman, *The Globalization Myth* (Icon Books, 2002)

The Hoover factory, built in west London in 1932, was an example of the new industries expanding in southern England and the Midlands while old industrial areas remained in the grip of depression and unemployment. Hoover vacuum cleaners were typical of the mass-produced electrical household goods that British consumers rushed to buy during this period.

6 War and Its Aftermath

New recruits, still in their civilian clothes, line up in front of a U.S. Army officer as America prepares for World War II. The entry of so many men into the armed forces in itself cut unemployment sharply, and equipping them for war gave a huge boost to industry.

World War II began in September 1939, when Nazi Germany invaded Poland, and Britain and France declared war on Germany in Poland's defense. Two years later, in December 1941, Japan attacked the U.S. naval base at Pearl Harbor, Hawaii, bringing America into the war.

Depression as a Cause of War

The Depression is generally recognized as one of the causes of World War II. It had helped to bring nationalists and militarists to power in Germany and Japan, the major aggressors in the war. Once in power, they had adopted a totally nationalist economic policy in response to the Depression. Since they did not want to be dependent on trade, instead seeking to become economically self-sufficient, they were tempted to plan the conquest of other countries that had resources they lacked. German dictator Hitler envisioned conquering a large area to the east of Germany and exploiting it to provide food for Germans. The Japanese wanted to control Indonesia, which was the source of most of Japan's oil supplies. Conquest also offered a solution to economic problems in a more direct way, since a defeated country could be plundered for its wealth and its people used as slave labor.

War Ends the Depression

If the Depression to some degree helped cause World War II, however, World War II in turn ended the Depression. In Britain, for example, unemployment had already fallen to 1 million by April 1940. By the following year serious labor shortages were developing, as millions of men and women were enrolled in the armed forces while, simultaneously, arms production expanded rapidly. British government spending went up from around 1 billion pounds in the last year of peace to almost 5 billion pounds in 1941–1942, giving a huge boost to the national economy. In the struggle for survival, the idea of balancing government income and expenditure was abandoned.

In the United States, unemployment started to fall sharply from 1939 onward. Even before America joined in the war, it became, in Roosevelt's words, "the arsenal of democracy," supplying arms and food to Britain and its allies. By the time of Pearl Harbor, 3 million Americans were unemployed, down from 9 million in 1939. Once the United States entered the war, unemployment was replaced by labor

VOICES FROM THE PAST

Good times in the war

World War II brought new prosperity to many Americans, including farmers who had experienced poverty in the 1920s and 1930s. A woman from rural Idaho remembered:

"As farm prices got better . . . we and most other farmers went from a tarpaper shack to a new frame house with indoor plumbing. Now we had an electric stove instead of a woodburning one, and running water at the sink where we could do the dishes; and a hotwater heater. . . . We bought a vacuum cleaner too . . . that was really wonderful!"

Quoted in David M. Kennedy, *Freedom from Fear* (Oxford University Press, 1999)

American B-24 Liberator bombers are built in a factory in the Midwest. Over 18,000 bombers of this type were manufactured during the war, an example of the astonishing feats of industrial mass production that contributed to the victory of the United States and its allies.

During the war, with so many American men in the armed forces and new factories opening every week, American companies were forced to recruit women to work in jobs in heavy industry, from which they had previously been excluded. When peace returned, most of them lost their wartime jobs.

shortages. As America's war industries boomed, workers were able to command higher wages. The availability of well-paid factory jobs attracted large numbers of poor farmers and farmworkers—many of them African Americans—to move to the cities. Women also broke into previously exclusively male areas of industrial work. By 1943, the United States was experiencing a boom not only in war industries but in the production of consumer goods, bought by workers with their rising wages. American industrial output doubled between 1939 and 1945.

Building a New World Order

Even before the war ended, the United States, Britain, and their allies started drawing up plans for the postwar world economy. They were determined that there would be no return to the Depression years. There would be internationalism, instead of the nationalism of the Depression era, and free trade instead of the use of tariffs to protect national economies. A new organization, the United Nations (UN), was to provide for international cooperation instead of conflict. The 1944 Bretton Woods Conference set up institutions under the UN umbrella to give order and stability to the world economy. The UN Charter listed employment as a fundamental human right—it was to be the duty of governments to prevent a return to mass unemployment.

By the end of the war, the United States was overwhelmingly the world's dominant economy, responsible for half of the world's total industrial output. While American industries had expanded and American living standards had risen, other industrialized countries on both sides in the war—including Germany, Japan, Britain, and the Soviet Union—had suffered large-scale destruction. In contrast to what

had happened after World War I, after 1945 the United States accepted the role of leader of the capitalist world economy. This was confirmed in 1947 when, under the Marshall Plan, the United States provided the money to help western European countries recover from the effects of the war. America's leaders understood that a general revival of the world economy would serve not only America's economic interests, but also its political interests since promoting prosperity was seen as a means of preventing the spread of communism.

TURNING POINT

Bretton Woods

In the summer of 1944, 730 delegates from 44 countries met at the American resort town of Bretton Woods, New Hampshire, to decide how the world economy should be run after the war. They were all determined that there should be no return to the Depression. The Bretton Woods Conference of July 1944 set up two key international institutions: the International Monetary Fund, to maintain stable exchange rates, and the International Bank for Reconstruction and Development (later to become the World Bank), to provide a stable source of capital investment to promote postwar economic recovery. The value of national currencies was to be fixed against the U.S. dollar, allowing global free trade to be restored. The Bretton Woods Conference established a stable system of international trade and finance after the war. The fixing of currencies against the dollar lasted until 1971.

The United Nations Security Council meets in New York in 1946. Although the Soviet Union and its allies were soon in a hostile relationship with the United States and its allies, the UN provided a useful framework for many kinds of international cooperation, including the promotion of free trade and economic recovery.

Women buy food at a drive-in restaurant in Los Angeles in 1951. In contrast to the Depression years of the 1930s, America in the 1950s was a place of prosperity and economic optimism, with steeply rising average incomes and low unemployment.

Postwar Boom

In the 1950s and 1960s, there was a sustained economic boom in the major industrial countries of western Europe, the United States, and Japan, with growth rates exceeding all expectations. Unemployment was low, trade flourished, and average incomes rose steeply. Economic and social policies varied from country to country, but all built to some degree on the lessons they had learned from the Depression. In both Europe and the United States, for example, governments supported agricultural prices by purchasing surplus farm produce or paying farmers to keep land out of production. Many countries were influenced by the ideas of British economist John Maynard Keynes, who said that governments should increase spending whenever there were signs of a rise in unemployment, to stimulate the economy and restore growth.

Fears for the Future

The return of economic troubles in the 1970s came as a shock to people who had come to see the problems of the Depression as part of the distant past. In 1971, the weakness of the dollar brought an end to the dollar-based fixed exchange rates agreed upon at Bretton Woods. Throughout the decade a mixture of high inflation and rising unemployment rocked industrial economies. In response, there was a return to the economic ideas of the pre-Depression era. Governments such as that of British prime minister Margaret Thatcher in the 1980s went back to the ideal of balancing budgets and cutting government spending. In the 1990s, much of the New Deal welfare system was abandoned in the United States.

Over the years there were periodic fears of a return to the Depression. In the 1980s, unemployment in some countries, including

HOW DID IT HAPPEN?

A return to the Depression

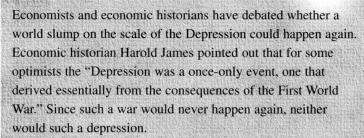

Economists and economic historians have debated whether a world slump on the scale of the Depression could happen again. Economic historian Harold James pointed out that for some optimists the "Depression was a once-only event, one that derived essentially from the consequences of the First World War." Since such a war would never happen again, neither would such a depression.

Historians Kevin O'Rourke and Jeffery Williamson, however, saw the Depression as having resulted from a "globalization backlash"—a nationalist reaction by key countries against the pre-1914 global economy, which they felt was harming their national interests. In this view, the globalized economy of the twenty-first century might again breed a hostile reaction from governments because of its inequalities and injustices, leading to a Depression-style breakdown in world trade.

Harold James, *The End of Globalization* (Harvard, 2001); Kevin O'Rourke and Jeffery Williamson, *Globalization and History* (MIT Press, 1999)

The Franklin D. Roosevelt Memorial in Washington, D.C., is visited by those who respect the memory of the architect of the New Deal—even if most of the welfare system he created had been abolished by the end of the twentieth century.

Britain, reached Depression-era levels. There were occasional stock market crashes that matched or even exceeded the Great Crash of 1929—notably in 1987 and at the start of the twenty-first century. But despite occasional setbacks, economic growth continued, and so did progress toward a global economy based on free trade and freedom of movement of capital. The memory of the Depression still stood as a warning of what human misery might result if that global economy ever fell apart.

THEY (WHO) SEEK TO ESTABLISH SYSTEMS OF GOVERNMENT BASED ON THE REGIMENTATION OF ALL HUMAN BEINGS BY A HANDFUL OF INDIVIDUAL [RUL]ERS . . . CALL THIS A NEW ORDER. [IT IS] NEW AND IT IS NOT ORDER.

The Great Depression Time Line

1914–1918 World War I fundamentally disrupts the world economy

1919 Peace treaty signed at Versailles imposes reparations payments on Germany

1921 Unemployment in Britain tops 2 million

1923 Hyperinflation in Germany destroys the value of the German currency

1929
March: Herbert Hoover is inaugurated as U.S. President
October 24: Share prices on the U.S. stock market crash on Black Thursday
October 29: Black Tuesday, the worst single day of the stock market crash

1930 Unemployment rises to 5 million in the United States; over 1,000 U.S. banks shut down

1931 Unemployment rises to over 5 million in Germany and over 3 million in Britain

1932 U.S. unemployment rises to 12–13 million; Franklin D. Roosevelt wins U.S. presidential election

1933
January 30: Nazi Party leader Adolf Hitler becomes chancellor of Germany
March–June: The first hundred days of Roosevelt's presidency lay the foundation for the New Deal
July: A World Economic Conference in London breaks up without agreement

1933–1935 Drought and soil erosion in Oklahoma and neighboring states create the dust bowl

1935 Radical measures of the Second New Deal are introduced, including the Social Security Act

1936
October: The Jarrow March of unemployed men brings a petition to the British Parliament
November: Roosevelt wins a landslide victory in presidential election

1937 Unemployment rises sharply again in the United States; a wave of sit-down strikes sweeps the United States; the Farm Security Administration is created to help the rural poor

1939 In September, World War II begins

1944 In July, the Bretton Woods Conference produces international agreement on how to organize a postwar world economy

Glossary

balanced budget A budget in which a government's spending equals its income
boom Sharp rise in economic activity
broker An agent who buys and sells on someone else's behalf
capitalism An economic system based on private ownership of business and trade

communism A system in which most or all economic life is controlled by the state
consumer goods Products sold to people for personal use
devaluing Reducing the value of one currency when exchanged for another
free (or private) enterprise Economic system based on the

pursuit of profit by individuals or companies
free trade International trade without excessive tariffs or obstructive regulations
global (or world) economy A single interlocking system of trade and investment
growth rates The speed at which an economy expands

hyperinflation A rise in prices so steep that a currency becomes virtually valueless

inflation A rise in prices and fall in the value of a currency

isolationism Tendency in the United States to avoid involvement in alliances or other entanglements with foreign countries

liberal capitalism A form of capitalism in which governments exercise an absolute minimum of control over economic activity

price-fixing agreement An arrangement between competing businesses not to sell goods below a certain price

shares A form of investment in business: People buy shares in companies and in theory make a profit if the company expands and increases in value

speculation Buying and selling shares in search of a quick profit, regardless of the true value of companies

stock market Place in which shares are traded

tariff A tax imposed on imported goods

Wall Street U.S. stock market

For Further Information

Books:

Karen Blumenthal, *Six Days in October: The Stock Market Crash of 1929*. New York: Atheneum, 2002.

Christopher Collier, *Progressivism, the Great Depression, and the New Deal, 1901 to 1941*. New York: Benchmark Books/Marshall Cavendish, 2001.

Michael L. Cooper, *Dust to Eat: Drought and Depression in the 1930s*. New York: Clarion, 2004.

Mary Gow, *The Stock Market Crash of 1929: Dawn of the Great Depression*. Berkeley Heights, NJ: Enslow, 2003.

R.G. Grant, *The Great Depression*. Hauppage, NY: Barron's, 2003.

Cory Gunderson, *The Great Depression*. Edina, MN: ABDO, 2004.

Alex Woolf, *The Wall Street Crash, October 29, 1929*. Chicago: Raintree, 2002.

Lisa A. Wroble, *The New Deal and the Great Depression in American History*. Springfield, NJ: Enslow, 2002.

Web Sites:

America from the Great Depression to WWII (http://memory.loc.gov/ammem/fsowhome.html)

Great Depression and WWII, 1929–1945 (http://memory.loc.gov/ammem/ndlpedu/features/timeline/depwwii/depwar.html)

New Deal Network (www.newdeal.feri.org)

Surviving the Dust Bowl (www.pbs.org/wgbh/amex/dustbowl)

Index

Page numbers in **bold** indicate photographs